Spare Scenes

Gillian P. Herbert

Copyright © 2012 by Gillian P. Herbert

All rights reserved. No part of this publication may be reproduced or transmitted in any form or by any means, electronic or mechanical, including photocopy, recording, or any information storage and retrieval system, without permission in writing from the publisher

Published in the United States by Gillian P. Herbert, Portland, Oregon

Requests for permission to make copies of any part of this work should be submitted to GPHwriter@gmail.com

The author is grateful to the editors of *Tiny Lights, Todd Point Review, Long Story Short, I Bleed Ink* and *ARRL* for publishing *Books, Footsteps, Full Circle (*which incorporated several *Spare Scenes* stories), *My Mother's Eyes, On Him,* and *A Cry in The Night* respectively. She would also like to express her gratitude to the judges of the Mendocino Writers Conference for awarding *Full Circle* 2nd place in creative non-fiction at their 2009 conference, and *Tiny Lights* for selecting *Footsteps* as a winner in their 2012 Flashpoint competition.

Credits:

Cover Photo: Brian Herbert
Photo Restoration: Rita Silverberg
Inside Photo: Rita Silverberg
Author Photo: Joan Bobkoff
Cover Design and Layout: Melody W. Baker

UP FRONT

Standing in front of the grey file cabinet, I contemplated the dusty manila folders and envelopes. Where to start? Whether to start at all? My parents were dead. All their paperwork had become my paperwork. I could close the drawer and walk away. Nobody would ever know I'd consigned their treasures to storage, to lie untouched and unexamined.

As I pulled out the first battered envelope, I muttered to myself, "One last job and then I can move on." I fingered a swatch of material and read the receipt for my mother's wedding dress. I turned the fabric over and puzzled at its colour— deep turquoise—until I remembered she had married only months after her father's death. Respect for the dead forbade wearing white while in mourning. I realised no one else would know: my mother's time-honoured gesture of respect would die with me.

Next, I flipped open a torn folder and rifled through a stack of yellowing sheets of paper. I scanned the paragraphs and recognised the irregular typeface of my father's portable typewriter. I folded myself into the nearest chair and began to read. I heard my father's voice strong and clear. The events he described—these were our family stories. How many times had I sat at my father's knee as he told these tales?

I carried the folder into the kitchen to brew a cup of tea. As I poured hot water into the teapot, I was struck with a sad realisation that I'd never hear these stories again. I was holding in my hands my parents' adventures, events they had magically woven into our family's memories. And, I held my own memorable moments, too, all of which would die with me, untold.

When I took out pen and paper and began reworking one of my father's scrappy tales, I watched it come alive. I became my parents' voices, telling their stories. Over time, as I added my own vivid memories from my family life, what emerged was this collection of spare scenes.

CONTENTS

Up Front	v
Act I: Back Stage	
A Cry in the Night	11
Frank	15
Teddy's Red Coat	19
Books	23
Tell Me!	25
Act II: Centre Stage	
On Time	31
Footsteps	35
My Mother's Eyes	39
Next Year	43
Muddy Knees	47
Line of Vision	51
"Make-Believe"	55
Too Far	57
Nothing Wrong	61
Crossroads	67
Like That	73
Yours	77
His Child	79
Not the Case	83
Like Gill	87
On Him	91

Act III: Curtain Call

A Shifting Shadow	97
Sotto Voce	101
Upper Hand	105
Too Late	109
The Gap	111
Off Limits	115
Not My Job	119
So Angry	123
Her Plan	125
Au Revoir	131
With Thanks	135
About the Author	137

ACT I:

BACK STAGE

A CRY IN THE NIGHT

At the beginning of September, 1939, Britain was about to engage in another European war. My father, as an early member of the Civilian Wireless Reserve formed by the Royal Air Force, knew he would be called up. He had already relocated his wife and their six-month old son to her parents' home near Cheltenham for safety.

Now he was rattling around alone in the barren and unwelcoming house in Bromley, Kent. He had packed and stored most of the household furniture and was down to clearing out the remaining debris. He wandered from room to room recalling happy family memories and storing them away against the impending chaos. He'd carried his bride over the threshold of this house, his son's arrival had marked the beginning of their family, these walls had seen much of their lives. He knew that the order to close down amateur radio stations would be issued shortly, so he had decided to pack up his gear. Outside, he had lowered the aerial at the corner of the house and tied it to the fence. The far end remained at the top of the 40-foot mast. He intended to leave it until the final order came to close down. His Sky Chief receiver was still in use and receiving signals on the 40-metre band. He listened idly as he gathered and packed radio components.

With nobody else at home he could go to

bed when he pleased. Thinking it was about time to do so, he gave the receiver dial a final twirl. He heard nothing of note until he paused at a station transmitting in hesitant French. He bent in close and put his ear to the speaker. It was a Polish station calling, *"Ici la station SP2AS,"* and *"Repondez-vous, s'il vous plait. Venez m'aider. C'est très importante."*

The Pole begged anyone who heard him to reply. My father sank into a chair and listened intently. He drummed his fingers on the table. His aerial wasn't hoisted to its normal height, and he doubted that with 10 watts of power he could reach the caller. But no one was responding. The pleas became more urgent and the voice more strident. *"Venez m'aider. Repondez-vous, s'il vous plait."*

My father switched on, tuned up, brought in the aerial and, summoning up his best classroom French, called back. *"C'est G2WI en Angleterre. Votre voix est très forte. Pouvez-vous m'entendre?"*

There was a heart-stopping pause. My father leant closer as he heard the Pole reply, *"G2WI, merci pour votre réponse. Moi situation est très dangereuse."*

He went on to say that the Germans were invading his country, pouring eastward in tanks and military vehicles. He could hear the thunder of their artillery and reckoned they would be at his house in half an hour. He cried out that he was in despair, and that soon he would be dead. When stuck for a word or expression, the man filled the gaps with, *"Vive l'Angleterre, vive la Pologne; vive votre famille."*

My father and the Pole talked earnestly for twenty minutes, until the Pole said he must stop, as the "military noises" were getting very, very close. My father leant back in his chair as he signed off, but immediately he heard a Swiss ham radio station, HB9CV, calling.

When he responded, the Swiss voice said, "I heard your entire QSL with the Pole. I regard it as a most historic contact, probably the last voice from free Poland. If you ever need confirmation of this contact, I shall be pleased to support you."

Wearily, my father unhooked his receiver and stashed it in a wooden crate. He wrapped the remainder of his equipment around the receiver, sat back in his chair, and gazed at the box for a long time. With reluctance, he nailed the lid closed. He knew British life was about to change dramatically, but didn't realize that it was going to be six turbulent years before he, together with the rest of the ham radio fraternity, would be free to speak once more to the world. Nor did he realize that despite efforts by him, by Polish Radio Amateurs and by the Polish Comrades Association, no trace would ever be found of the ham radio operator using SP2AS as his call sign.

FRANK

In September, 1941, my father was posted to Canada to teach servicemen how to operate the radio equipment in English fighter planes. Canada was supporting the British RAF by flying their airmen to England. The pilots had no problem transferring their skills from Canadian to British planes, but the radio operators needed a four-week training program. For wartime, four weeks was too long for planes and pilots to be idle. Instructors like my father were given the challenge to make this training shorter. My father arrived in Patricia Bay on Vancouver Island in December, when the snow was deep and the air biting cold. He was on the last leg of his journey from London. He'd flown the Atlantic, crossed Canada by train, taken a rough ferry ride, and ridden a local army truck to the airbase. Once on base, he was informed he'd be billeted with a local family. He was given instructions on their location, shouldered his kit bag and accepted the loan of a Jeep.

Half an hour later he realized he was lost, so he pulled over at a crossroads. There were few homes, so he slogged through knee-high snow to the nearest, a bungalow, where he climbed the front steps to the porch. A woman came to the door and he asked for directions to Mrs. McVie's cabin. They were very complicated, and she could tell from his bewildered expression that he had no idea where to go. As Dad turned away, she said, "There's an old gentleman here who's going that way. He'll show you the road, if you'll give him a lift."

Grateful, my dad agreed, and she turned back into the house and called, "Mr. Herbert, there's an airman here who is going your way and will give you a lift."

The hair on my dad's neck stood on end, but he remained silent. Out came a white-haired, spry old boy and together they climbed into the Jeep and started off up the track.

"Your name's Herbert?" said my dad. "That's a good old-fashioned English name."

"I came from England forty-seven years ago," the old man replied. "From a little village outside London called Camberwell."

Daddy told him that Camberwell was now part of London, and then asked, "Where did you live in Camberwell?"

"Asylum Road."

"Do you have any brothers or sisters?"

"I was one of seven brothers and one sister."

Dad pulled the Jeep to an abrupt stop and looked over at his companion. "And that sister, her name was Elsie."

The old man paled. "How do you know?"

"Your name is Frank and your eldest brother is Ted. And I know because Ted was my father. I grew up hearing about how you went to sea as a young lad and were never heard from again."

After my mother and brother joined my father in Pat Bay, Uncle Frank spent time with the family. Though he told stories of his many adventures, we never learnt why he left England. Nor why he didn't stay in touch with his family. When the war ended and we returned to England, we never heard from him again.

TEDDY'S RED COAT

The snow was piled against the walls and steps of the lonely cabin. Moonlight cast deep shadows on the land and reflected off the waters of Patricia Bay, Vancouver Island. In its rawness, the land looked untouched and beautiful, a few snow-brushed trees breaking the horizon. All was quiet and crisp.

Inside, our mother listened to my brother, Ian, who lay curled up in his bed reciting his night-time prayers. He ended with "And thank you for the new red coat Santa is bringing for Teddy."

My mother's heart dropped, her face grew impassive and her mind raced. In this era of wartime shortages, in this distant and isolated place, she had worked so hard to fulfil Ian's wish list which included a red wagon and coloured crayons. She knew nothing of a red coat for Teddy. My mother walked to the window and stared out. Her forehead rested against the cold glass and tears slid down her face. It was too hard, being six thousand miles from home, in a foreign country, in a rustic cabin, out of town. When my father had been posted to Patricia Bay Air Force Base, she had immediately applied for passage to join him. This was a rare opportunity to take our family to safety, away from the nightly bombing raids over London. She and Ian had sailed to Canada on the last wartime voyage of the Queen Mary. The Germans had blown the prow off the boat and it was to be dry-docked for repairs in the safety of Canada. The ship was overcrowded with evacuated women and children. Conditions were primitive and chaotic: cabin doors had been removed for easy access, and four families shared each cabin which held four bunk beds. Lurking German enemy submarines kept everyone aware of the threat of being torpedoed.

After they docked in Montreal, my mother and brother travelled across Canada by train. Four days later they reached Vancouver Island and were reunited with my father. The journey had been an ordeal for this quiet country woman. Despite missing her family, she finally felt safe from the day-to-day strain of bombing raids. She turned away from the window, tucked in her son and closed his door quietly as she went to her bedroom. She and my father readied themselves to brave the snow drifts and walk to the "big" house nearby, where they were to join the McVie family for Christmas Eve festivities. Since my mother's arrival, the McVies had generously provided the cabin for shelter, the firewood for warmth, and on many days, afternoon tea for companionship.

My mother mingled with the guests, smiled bravely and chatted politely. Suddenly, she felt a light touch on her arm.

"Gladys, what's wrong? You look worried," Annie McVie asked.

"Nothing," she replied. "It was just Ian's last-minute request to Santa, and I had no idea."

"What was it?"

"A red coat for his teddy bear. Ian thinks Santa is bringing Teddy a new coat. There's nothing I can do now."

"We'll see about that!"

Annie called to her teenage daughters and explained Ian's request.

This British three-year-old, with his precise English accent and polite manners, had won the hearts of the McVie daughters. They leapt to respond. With enthusiasm and laughter they whipped out knitting needles and an old red sweater. Together, they pulled yarn from the sweater and their needles began to click. My mother watched speechlessly as these young women knitted, sewed and pressed a small red coat. When it was finished, they wrapped it protectively from the falling snow.

With care, my mother tucked the package under her coat and trudged back to the cabin. She lifted the teddy bear from her son's bed, slipped on the red coat and propped the bear up, so Ian would see it when he awoke.

That last request fulfilled, my mother sank back into the rocking chair, pulled the blanket around herself, and watched the snow drifting down. Relaxed now, she was content to doze, to wait and watch for daybreak.

BOOKS

The three of us walked briskly up the hill towards the park. The day was sunny but crisply cold. We all wore heavy jackets and gloves. Mother had a thick scarf pulled around her head and shoulders; her dark brown eyes peered out from its layers. She kept me tethered to her with my bright red leather 'trainer' reins. As we neared the park, Mother reminded us, "You can go into the park and watch the ducks while I choose books in the library. Ian, you're to watch Gill and look after her. I won't be long." Ian took my reins and we scurried towards the pond.

As mother stood in the library browsing the shelves, her mind left hearth and home and travelled to distant lands and other worlds. English literature was her first love and, in teacher training college in 1929, she had studied it as her major. She planned to teach high school students when she graduated. But, during her first year, she took a required practicum in an elementary school with a classroom of five-year-olds. At the close of the term the school headmistress approached her and asked if she would join her staff when she graduated. "You have a natural talent with the little ones."

Mother was grateful for the offer. These were the Depression years and jobs were very scarce. But her heart fell as she watched her dream slide away. No exciting discussions of worthy books, no essays to mark. After graduation, she accepted the position, but with much sadness.

In the library, her eyes travelled the shelves as she sought her favourite authors. Suddenly, a cry pierced her quiet journey through the stacks.

"Does anyone have a little girl in a red outfit?" Her heart trembled as she shrank into the book stacks, desperately wishing to be invisible. And then she raced outside. There I stood, mud from head to waist, crying. My brother stood beside me, also crying.

"I tried, Mummy, I really tried, but I couldn't pull her up; she was too heavy. I told her not to lean over so far but she wouldn't listen." Bystanders had grabbed the reins and pulled me from the mud.

My mother told my brother, "Run home quickly and tell Daddy to run a warm bath." She followed him, her hands heavy with a muddy child, but no books.

TELL ME!

My mother walked slowly out the hospital's swinging doors and down the steps, then climbed into the car my father had just pulled in to the kerb.

"Brian, what are we going to do? Gill is not getting better, and now she won't eat unless I'm there to feed her."

Daddy looked across at Mummy and saw the deep lines etched into her forehead and the tears in her eyes. She was exhausted. He ran his fingers through his hair. He said nothing. He had nothing to offer.

Two years earlier, at the end of the war, my family had returned to England from Canada. Daddy had been demobilised from the RAF, and my parents returned to teaching. My brother, Ian, was settled in a local primary school, and I played every day in the nursery school class my mother taught. But, much of the time, I was sick and either at home or in hospital. The change to the humid, foggy chill of England was too much for my young lungs. One bronchial illness followed another, and even holidays were interrupted and cut short. Mummy and Daddy worked hard to keep our family life intact, but daily hospital treks were wearing them down.

On this day, my father put the car into first gear

and pulled away from the kerb. "There's not much else we can do."

Next day, Daddy left school during his lunch hour and popped over to the hospital for a quick visit. He strode through the hallways to the open ward where I lay. He heard none of the noises around him: the clanging of metal equipment, the moaning of sick children, the soft words of anxious parents. As he walked past the beds, he saw only me, curled on my side with strands of hair sticking to my sweaty forehead, a little girl barely able to smile. He passed his hand over his face to hide his tears and fears; his little one was so sick.

Daddy lifted me into his arms and felt my frailty. Turning from my bed, he carried me out the ward and down the corridors towards the sun lounge, where he wanted to sit in one of the big rocking chairs and rock me while whispering words of love and comfort. Rounding the corner into the sun room, he came face-to-face with our family doctor, Dr. Lyntton Low. Without any niceties, he blurted out, "What do I have to do to make this child well? Tell me what to do!"

She looked at him over her gold-rimmed glasses. "Take her to a warm climate, a hot climate where her lungs can heal—and stay there a long time."

Daddy said nothing. The anger drained from his face as he sank into the rocker. He knew the advice was sound. He also knew that they didn't have the resources to take me to the sun. His chin rested on my head.

Dinner that evening was a sombre meal. Mummy had laid out the food, but taken herself off to bed early. The daily grind of teaching for eight hours and then going to the hospital to feed me was wearing her out. She needed to lie down. Ian ate with a book propped up against the cruet, while Daddy distracted himself by scanning the newspapers and the weekly *Times Education Supplement.* Suddenly, he froze, and then forced his eyes back to the beginning of the advertisement:

> *Headmaster for Senior school*
> *Headmistress for Primary school.*
> *Qualified staff needed for the above positions for*
> *schools on a joint military base in Ismailia, Egypt.*

We sailed for the Middle East three months later. My lungs healed.

ACT II:

CENTRE STAGE

ON TIME

As a child, my whole world ran on a clearly defined, predictable schedule. Routine was a major part of my family life; the regularity and reliability of our days gave me great comfort. Because both my parents were school teachers, and my brother and I were students, we shared the same schedule: two weeks holiday for Christmas, two weeks for Easter, and six weeks in the summer. Each morning my father dropped us off at our schools and picked us up again in the evening. Our weekend activities also fell into a familiar routine. Saturday mornings my father worked on the car, my brother gardened, my mother and I cooked. Saturday afternoon was reserved for shopping in town. Sunday mornings were for quiet or church time. Sunday afternoons and evenings were for naps and "read-a-book" times. Our lives followed a reassuring timetable.

Even if it was leisure time, promptness was important. We all understood that we needed to be on time in order to function cooperatively. Not only did I know that promptness was good manners, I also thought this was how the world worked. None of this seemed unreasonable to me; it just was the way my family functioned.

Many years later, I sat in my mother's bedroom listening to her talk about my father's memory loss. She confided that friends had visited recently and he'd monopolized the conversation with old war stories.

"I just want him to talk about our lives," she said. "Of the adventures we had together. And, today I wish he'd told you some of the events of our family you may not remember."

"Mummy," I told her, understanding her frustration. "Why don't you tell me one of the stories?"

"Well, there's that day in Ismailia when you went missing."

I sat back, a little startled. I remembered being six and living in Egypt. My parents ran the school on the British military base and I went to a weekly ballet class taught by a French woman. I didn't like ballet much. I was of stocky build, and felt clumsy when compared to the other children. But there weren't too many activities in Egypt for European children, so my parents insisted I participate.

When class was over, I would unleash my ballet shoes and shrug off my dance outfit with glee. I'd run downstairs, and out the main door where I'd wait at the top of the steps leading to the street. I'd hang out with the other children waiting for their rides, and we'd chat and throw our ballet shoes in the air and play around. I always waited patiently because I could hear my father's reminder, "If you get lost, just stand still and wait, and we will find you." Usually Mummy and Daddy were the first to arrive, and I'd leap into the car and we'd drive to the beach.

In the town of Ismailia, there was little that was green. Sandy dunes, rough dirt roads, and screamingly white buildings were everywhere. But I knew that only miles away was Lake Timsah with beautiful beaches and cold blue water. Young soldiers had moored rafts some distance out, and I loved to swim over where they'd haul me up and toss me far out into the lake. This is where I spent every afternoon when the temperature soared over 100°. It was my reward for enduring school that started at six in the morning and ran until one in the afternoon.

"So, what happened when I went missing?" I asked my mother.

"Your father and I were supposed to pick you up at four o'clock, but we ran late and suddenly it was four-twenty. We rushed out of the flat, leapt into the car, and your father drove a little recklessly to the far side of the French quarter. When we drew up outside, you weren't there. 'Don't worry,' I told your father, 'She's probably inside with the teacher. It's so hot out here.'

We ran up the stairs and went straight to your classroom. Bursting into the room, your father called out, 'We're here to pick up Gill. Where is she?' The teacher turned from the piano and shook her head. 'She left with the rest,' she said. 'Isn't she outside?' Just then her phone rang.

'Oui, oui. Vraiment. Merci beacoup,' she said as she turned back to us and said, 'That was a neighbour. She just saw a soldier and a little girl walking down

the passageway next to this building. The child was carrying ballet shoes.'

Your father sprinted to the door and yelled back over his shoulder for me to call the MPs and tell them it was an emergency. He vaulted down the stairs, threw himself through the front door, and raced towards the passageway. Frantically he ran from doorway to doorway, courtyard to courtyard. Finally, turning into an inner courtyard, he saw you. Your knees seemed ready to buckle, and your body sagged as you stood, head cast down, arms wrapped around yourself. Your ballet shoes hung limply in your hand. Brian said he sprinted forward, shouldered the soldier out of the way, and swept you into his arms. Meanwhile, I stood out on the front steps after directing the Military Police towards the back of the buildings. The police took off at a run with their heavy boots clattering on the cobblestones.

I lifted my head at the sound of slow, heavy footsteps and saw your father carrying you, talking gently as you nestled your head up under his chin. I ran to him, hugged you both, and then we went to the beach for a swim. You were just fine."

With this, my mother got up and went off to reheat the water for the tea pot. I knew I'd never know what, if anything, happened in that courtyard. That wasn't our way. But I did know why we were never late.

FOOTSTEPS

The white roof shimmered under a relentless sun. Washing lines, uncharacteristically empty, swayed in the breeze. Inside the building, my brother and I peered around the door.

"Nobody out here," called out Ian. "Come on, Gill."

We scrambled out and skittered to the low wall surrounding the roof. The heat seeped through our sandals. We crouched in the shelter of the wall and listened.

In 1951, we were living in a block of flats that stood in the heart of Ismailia's European quarter. The flats faced a large green park, beyond which ran the sweet water canal. We'd lived there for three years and found the locals friendly and welcoming, but civil unrest had been growing from resentment over the British control of the Suez Canal.

For the previous two weeks, my brother, father, and I had remained barricaded in our flat as rioting flared in the streets around us. The windows were shuttered and our furniture stacked against the front door. Our only links to the outside were our faithful houseboy, Esseden, who came each night under cover of darkness to leave food at the back door, and Daddy's unlicensed ham radio equipment. Every day, Daddy sent messages back to Mummy telling her we were safe. She was in England, recuperating from ear surgery necessitated by a sudden loss of hearing.

Ian and I helped to prepare our meals and Daddy kept us entertained with stories, games and homework. Many days of house restriction had made us stir-crazy so we hatched a plan. We would wait until Daddy was on the air then we'd slip up the back stairs to the roof and see what was happening outside. Ian was twelve and I eight, and it never occurred to us that this escapade might be risky.

From the shelter of the wall Ian gave me a boost and together we gazed out, keeping our heads low.

"Look," I pointed. "Those two buildings are on fire."

My brother pointed to lorries that were upside down, as well as a burning car. We hung there quietly, taking in the scene. Suddenly, three Egyptians dashed around the corner, gallibayas flying out behind them, as they ran across the park. More Egyptians, in police uniforms, chased after them. We heard yelling and motors running and engines backfiring.

"Ian, the front man fell down. And another."

"Get up! Get up!" we yelled in unison, just as strong hands grabbed us by the collar and pulled us off the wall. Daddy's white, strained face expressed the severity of our adventure. Crawling on all fours, he pushed us across the roof to the stairs. We ran down and in through the back door. My brother and I sat on the kitchen floor and waited for the axe to fall. Much to our surprise, Daddy said nothing. He poured glasses of water and gave them to us before sitting on the floor with us.

"Gill," he told me, "those men can't get up because they are dead. That popping noise was gunfire. They've been shot." I curled my knees up to my chest and hugged them. Ian went pale and stared at the floor.

"It's very dangerous outside," he continued. "Neither the Egyptian nor the British army can control the rioting and people are getting hurt. We have to stay safe until the British army can come get us." He reached out and pulled us close. "I know it's hard and you've really been helping me, but we have to hang on a little longer." He smiled at us.

We were getting to our feet when we heard the shattering of glass, the sounds of running feet and then yelling.

"They've broken through the main doors!" said Dad. "Quick, we have to hide."

Ian and I ran to the living room and crawled into the kneehole under an old roll-top desk. Daddy yanked open a drawer, pulled out his service revolver, and followed us under the desk. Jammed up tight against one another, my father's arms held us as his hand held the gun.

Sounds of splintering wood and crashing furniture grew louder, and then feet were thumping through the flat empty below. Within seconds, footsteps were pounding up one more flight, and there was banging on our door. We watched transfixed as our door shook, but the stacked furniture held it firm. I cried quietly into Daddy's neck.

More yelling, and then the blows shifted to the flat next door. The wood cracked and broke as the men ran in shouting wildly. Suddenly, a shrill, piercing scream ripped the air, followed by several more. Footsteps clattered back down and out.

The building fell silent. We sat very still. We'd survived. But we knew the mother and son who lived next door had not.

MY MOTHER'S EYES

It was the Sunday before Christmas and we were all scurrying around, checking that everything was ready for our guests. Each year at this time my parents invited the entire staff from their schools to come for a gathering. It was usually a joyous, sometimes even raucous, crowd.

Outside, the snow was swept from the path and street lights gleamed through the falling flakes. Inside, my mother and I had been working feverishly in the kitchen all afternoon. Often we had a difficult time working together, due to her loss of hearing. By now she barely heard a word, so I communicated with hand gestures. It was becoming harder for us to understand each other. At age ten, I wanted to please her so much, although her detached glances told me I rarely succeeded. But we had prepared a grand traditional afternoon tea together so often that I knew what to do. Occasionally, she would smile and point at a plate or a knife, but for the most part we just worked side by side in companionable silence. On this day, I felt her approval and basked in it.

My father had spent days decorating the house with garlands and brightly coloured pennants he had collected in Canada. Our tree stood in the bay window, covered with twinkling lights, glimmering icicles and decorations. A pile of presents sat underneath.

Footsteps crunched on the icy snow, as the guests carefully made their way up the steps and pathways to the house. I ran to the door. I was proud of the responsibility given me to open it, welcome my parents' friends, take their wet coats, and send them into the living room. Meanwhile, my mother hurried around in the kitchen putting the finishing touches to this teatime feast, as my father held court in the living room. His job was to entertain until everyone had arrived.

The entire gathering moved into the dining room where an elaborate afternoon tea was served. I had laid the table with a linen cloth, and put out small knives and forks along with dessert plates and serviettes. I had also put the teapot, cups and saucers, teaspoons and milk and sugar on the tea trolley, just as my mother had taught me. In the kitchen were plates of tiny sandwiches filled with egg salad or ham or cream cheese and cucumber, buttered scones, mince pies, tarts and cakes.

As folk settled into armchairs my mother brewed the tea and wheeled the trolley into the dining room. I handed everyone a plate, serviette and small fork, and then made my way around offering plates of food, while the guests sat and talked. My mother was busy pouring and passing out cups of tea, topping up the pot with hot water, and refilling cups. I spent much time running around ensuring that everybody had a full plate. Suddenly, I realised all the sandwiches were gone and I turned to my mother. Would she be annoyed if I pointed this out? I took the empty plate to her which she whisked away to the kitchen, returning with a back-up plate from the larder. She smiled gently at me and I sighed with relief.

After tea, my father took the men back into the living room, where they settled in and partook of hard liquor and cigarettes or cigars. The women helped my mother carry everything to the kitchen and then they regrouped in the dining room for one last cup of tea. Most of the women had known my mother for years and knew how to communicate with her. Since my part was over, I was free to go to my bedroom, where I worked on a jigsaw puzzle and listened to Christmas carols on my radio. The sounds of chatter and rounds of laughter floated up from downstairs.

Later, I went down to ask my mother's help with my puzzle. I slipped through the half-open door and saw how her high-backed wing chair was angled so her back was to me. She was wearing a high-necked, wine-coloured dress that she saved for holiday gatherings. I stood near her as she smiled and spoke to her guests. They were listening attentively to this beautiful woman with warm brown eyes and jet-black hair plaited and worn in a bun. She had high cheekbones and naturally rosy colouring. I knew she hadn't seen, and her deafness prevented her from hearing, me.

I stood silently, waiting for a break in the conversation. Then she said, "I am convinced that when two academically gifted people, two intelligent people, have children, one of them is gifted and the other is not." As she spoke, her guests shot me quick glances. I turned bright red. My older brother was a scholarship student. That left me the mediocre one in my mother's eyes. Quietly I turned and left the room. I went back to my bedroom and closed the door firmly. I turned off my radio and put away my jigsaw puzzle. I changed into my pyjamas and crawled into bed. I lay trembling, even though I wasn't cold. Hiding under the covers, I recalled all the cold, distant glances my mother had given me over the years. Now I knew why.

NEXT YEAR

I struggled from beneath my blankets and peered over my toes, looking for the pillowcase I knew would be at the foot of my bed. The room was filled with shadows outlined in many shades of gray; dim, early-morning light skittered around the curtains: it wasn't yet six o'clock. I kept still and listened but heard nothing. The house was very quiet. But I knew it was Christmas morning and that the pillowcase would be stuffed with Santa's best: toys, books, socks, oranges and nuts, all in a wild assortment of colour, surprise, and delight. I had no idea how hard my mother had worked all year to squirrel away these gifts. This was post-World War II England, a country awash in pain and deprivation and pride. And it was this very pride that drove my mother to make sure her children enjoyed the full and wondrous experience of Christmas. Throughout the year, wherever she went, she sought out the small gifts that she and my father would wrap in bright red and green paper and load into the pillowcases for Santa, who would sneak into our bedrooms and leave them at the foot of our beds.

Downstairs, in the living room, sat our brightly lit Christmas tree. We'd all spent the previous afternoon decorating it. Mother had hung the many ornaments we'd collected as we travelled the world, while my brother Ian wound long, swirling, silver garlands between the branches. Daddy had played carols on the piano as I'd jostled between Mummy and Ian to thread silver tinsel from every tree limb. The final step was for Daddy to lug in a ladder, climb it and attach the gold star on the uppermost branch.

I knew there would be a pile of wrapped gifts under the tree. These were the serious gifts – the educational or useful gifts – books, jigsaws and clothing. These were to be opened after breakfast, once the turkey was in the oven. We'd all gather around the tree, Mummy and Daddy with their cups of morning coffee, and Ian and I to read the labels and carry the gifts to each person. Gradually, next to each chair, a pile would grow. Once all the gifts were distributed, we would take turns opening them. Time would be spent laughing and chatting.

On this Christmas morning, my eyes flew open. My pillowcase was there, as I'd known it would be! I also knew that Mummy and Daddy, weary from teaching the autumn term, and now preparing for Christmas festivities, were fast asleep. It was our long-standing family tradition that when they awoke, Dad would call out, inviting us kids, still in our pyjamas, into their room. There, we would curl up at the foot of their bed with our pillowcases and open our gifts, while they watched in enjoyment.

I thought of my brother in his room next door. *Maybe he was awake?* I crawled out of bed, and in bare feet, padded to his bedside. I shook his shoulder gently.

"Ian, Ian, wake up."

Startled, he jumped at my touch. "What's up, Gill?"

"Nothing. Everything. Ian, it's Christmas."

He grinned and ruffled my hair. "Are Mum and Dad awake?"

"No. But our pillowcases are here."

He grinned again.

"Let's take them downstairs and open some gifts," I said. "If we're quiet, they won't hear us."

Grinning once more, he nodded.

I crept back to my room, pulled on my slippers, and carried my pillowcase onto the landing. Ian appeared in his dressing gown, with his pillowcase slung over his shoulder. We made it down the stairs as far as the first landing, and then impatience won out. Sinking to our knees, we fished around for the first gift. As we unearthed the treasures, we tried to stifle our laughter, but each new gift brought more excitement. Ultimately, we gave in to smothered giggling and snorts of laughter.

Then Ian went quiet. I followed his gaze and saw my father standing at the top of the stairs. He didn't say anything. For a second we froze, before creeping back up the stairs in silence. We held hands as we inched our way around Dad without touching him, and turned into our rooms. Back in bed, I crawled under my blankets and lay for a long time listening to my parents. The rustle of wrapping paper and their footsteps up and down the stairs told me they were gathering up the debris and gifts and placing them under the Christmas tree. Some while later, my bedroom door swung open and my father crossed the room to put a cup of tea down beside my bed.

"Breakfast is ready, get up and come on downstairs."

We all ate together, in near silence.

After Ian and I had cleared the table and washed the dishes, we all trooped into the living room and opened the gifts under the tree. It was a muted gathering. In the empty space somehow I knew, as the one responsible for the morning's escapade, that I was in serious trouble. My mother barely smiled and, when she spoke, her sentences were short and terse. She pretty much ignored me. The rest of the day was quiet too.

The next year there were no pillowcases. Nothing was said. We just knew. All our presents were under the Christmas tree, the foot of our beds bare. My brother and I were grown up now.

MUDDY KNEES

My favourite time was Saturday morning, when I was free to play outdoors. Clad in my brother's outgrown school clothes—grey wool shorts, knee high socks, and V-necked pullover—I scrambled about resurrecting my fort. Built of scrap lumber, broken glass, and old tin cans, it served as the perfect background for the battles I played out with my brother's lead soldier figures. The rain had washed away the mud ramparts, burying most of the soldiers, and the moat was flooded. I was getting pretty mucky, but I didn't care.

Suddenly, I heard my father's voice: "Gill, come in and wash your hands. We're going for a ride."

I leapt up happily. Where we went didn't matter. I loved solo jaunts in the car with my dad.

As we drove across south London, we chatted about school and friends and plans for our summer holiday. This year, it was to be a road trip to Kent where we'd stay "en famille" on a country farm. I was excited at the prospect of herding cows, collecting fresh-laid eggs, and riding horses. A farm provided "on-site entertainment" for my brother and me, so our parents could get some rest.

Eventually, Daddy parked the car on a side street outside a red school building and told me, "I'm going to take you in with me. I have to go and talk to someone for a while. You need to sit patiently and wait."

I nodded. My father was a school principal who often went to important meetings at various schools. Sitting quietly was a small price to pay for riding with him.

This particular school was very old. A flight of grey marble steps led up to double wooden doors, which were flanked by huge white pillars. Inside, the ceilings were high and the quietness alarming. I held tight to Daddy's hand. He found the school secretary, who led us to an office. I was told to wait outside, so I sat on a metal chair. The corridor was painted grey with a black and white tile floor, and flights of stairs seemed to float off in every direction.

The door opened and my father came out saying, "Gill, wait in here with Miss Pearse. I'll be back soon."

I got up and trotted through the door into a large, quiet room. A big desk sat at an angle in front of blue velvet curtains that partially obscured the windows. Three armchairs were around a coffee table near the fireplace and a gas fire sputtered. A woman smiled and invited me to sit with her near the fire. She lifted a box of foreign postage stamps onto the table and asked me to help sort them. I was glad I'd washed my hands properly. Muddy knees and scuffed shoes didn't faze me, but dirty hands would have been an embarrassment.

The stamps opened up a conversation about living abroad and we chatted away. We talked of other countries I might visit one day and the school subjects that taught me about these places. I was just realizing that this was more fun than I usually had while waiting for Daddy, when I heard the door open. My father stood there, looking directly over my head at Miss Pearse. I turned just in time to see her nod her head and say, "Yes, of course."

Daddy called me to him and we left the building. As we drove home, he wanted to know about my stamp sorting, so I proudly recounted my conversation with Miss Pearse. I asked if I could visit her again so I could work on the stamps some more. He smiled.

Back home, I ran to the garden to continue working on my fort, but my father called me back. "Gill, I think we'd better go in and tell your mother where we've been."

We walked into the kitchen where my mother was putting the finishing touches to our lunch. She welcomed us with a smile and asked, "What have you two been up to?"

"I took Gill to the Mary Datchelor Girls' School for an interview with the school principal."

My mother's eyes grew big and she grabbed the edge of the table. "How could you? Why didn't you tell me?"

"Gladys, you know we've tried to get her into so many grammar schools that wouldn't even consider her because they were full. Datchelor is one of the top London schools. It was a big chance, but I knew that if I could get her in the door, she'd win them over. I phoned the school secretary and asked for ten minutes with the principal to discuss a bright student. I was told that if I went right away the principal would see me, as she was working in her office this morning. Once there, I confessed it was Gill, and Miss Pearse laughed and said, 'Well, you've brought her so I may as well see her'. And she did. And Gill won her over: she's been accepted!"

My mother sank into her little rocking chair and looked at me. I was dirty and unkempt, but with a beaming smile. "You took her like that?" she declared. "All muddy and dirty? She had a school interview looking like that?"

LINE OF VISION

"No, absolutely not. Remove that immediately."
"I think not."
"Immediately."

They stared at each other from across a hospital bed. Stiff white sheets covered my brother, who lay motionless. Only his eyes moved, flitting back and forth, tracking the harsh words.

"I'm sorry, but I think not." My mother held the gaze of the white-coated doctor. "If you consider for a moment, you will recall the reason why my son lies desperately ill in this hospital. He is here because of your staff's error."

With these words, my mother swept all three of them back to the events of the preceding weeks. Our family had been staying on a farm at Ashford, in Kent. Ian and I had spent our days collecting eggs, herding cows and bringing in the harvest. My parents were able to rest and recoup from a year of teaching.

Several weeks into our stay, my parents and I returned home so that mother could attend medical appointments with her hearing specialist. It was believed that Ian, at fourteen, was old enough to stay on the farm. The farmer's wife reassured my parents that she would treat him like her own. The only rule was that Ian was not to go game hunting without the farmer.

All was well until Ian and the farmer's son secretly

went duck hunting. The farmer's son later recounted that Ian stumbled and fell. The shotgun fired, and the lead pellets tore through his left foot. Frantic, the farmer's boy ran for help. The farmer carried Ian to his car and drove him to hospital where his wounds were treated. Back at the farm, a tearful Ian phoned Mummy and Daddy and owned up. They were furious and forbade him to leave the farmhouse until we returned two days later.

As we drove towards the farm gate, we were met by the farmer, who informed us very seriously, "Ian's not so good. He ran a fever. He went back into hospital this morning."

We sped back through country lanes into Ashford and straight to the hospital. There, we learnt Ian was seriously ill. He had developed tetanus, more commonly known as lockjaw, because the emergency room staff who'd cleaned his wound hadn't given him a tetanus vaccination.

For the next three weeks, my mother sat at Ian's bedside. She assisted in his care, washing and turning him, and reminded him of stories from his childhood. Daddy and I went back home because the autumn term was starting at his school. On Friday nights, we'd drive to join Mother and we'd all sit with Ian, who was paralyzed. He could move his eyes, nothing more. When we talked to him, he'd watch our lips, but he had no way to respond. The doctor informed us that Ian was losing ground, he was giving up, and there was no more they could do.

Mother told of sitting there, day after day, watching Ian. One morning, she noticed his eyes tracking. What was he watching? She followed his gaze and realised he was focused on a fly. Ian told later, "I had nothing else to do, so I followed the fly." When Mummy returned the next day, his eyes were still and unresponsive. She searched the room. The fly was gone.

Anger welled up in my mother, she felt helpless. Her son was going to die. She ran from the room, down the hall to the ward sister's desk, where she grabbed the phone. Urgently, she called for a taxi. As she climbed into the cab she said, "Take me to the pet store. Any one will do. And hurry."

An hour later, a somewhat bemused taxi driver delivered her back to the hospital. He parked his cab outside and followed my mother through long, sterile corridors to Ian's room. There, he gently lowered a fish tank, complete with gravel, rocks, plants and fish, onto the bedside table. Mummy wheeled it round and placed it directly in Ian's line of vision. For a second he didn't respond, then his eyes opened wide and darted back and forth, following the fish. Mummy sank into a chair and breathed deeply. Ian had a fighting chance.

Suddenly, the door flew open and the doctor marched in.

"No. Absolutely not. Remove that immediately."
"I think not."
The tank stayed. Ian recovered completely.

"MAKE-BELIEVE"

Chatter and laughter filled the school assembly hall. Built in the late 1800s, it was large enough to seat over six-hundred pupils, all the staff and the parents of the First Form. It was an annual tradition for each year's class to perform a play. The older girls staged a Shakespearean play, but the eleven year-olds were considered too young for such complex work, so the drama teacher chose a more suitable piece.

That year, it was "Oliver's Island" by A.A. Milne. After weeks of rehearsing, the cast was set to perform. My mother sat on the edge of her seat.

The curtain rose to the opening set of a schoolroom. A schoolboy lay on the floor, reading a book. As the action moved forward, Oliver told his sister of a fantasy island he'd created in his mind where he retreated when he didn't like a lesson or believed their governess was being too harsh. His sister asked to go to Oliver's island, and the audience was led into a play within a play that included shipwrecks, pirates, battles and buried treasure.

We made it through the entire performance with a minimum of forgotten lines and miscues. As we lined up for our curtain calls, we were beaming with pride. The applause was so enthusiastic we knew we had done a good job.

As my mother rose to leave, she was greeted by the school headmistress, Miss Pearse. "Mrs. Herbert,

Gillian really did so well. One would never have known Oliver was a girl!"

Mummy smiled awkwardly. "She did, didn't she?"

"Yes, and in those grey wool shorts, knee-high socks and V-necked pullover she was just the part. She looked so natural, but I'm not so sure it was really 'make-believe'!"

Mummy nodded her head. "I'm afraid not."

TOO FAR

The beach stretched away from us: long, smooth golden sand. Situated on the craggy coast of Cornwall, it was a favourite for families on holiday. The sand, which backed up to towering rocks, was dotted with family clusters, with each area staked out, delineated by towels, chairs, umbrellas and bags. A small gravel road, running along the rocks at one end of the beach, was strewn with parked cars, ice cream stalls and many vendors. Young children ran in and out of the water, splashing and giggling. A group of teens swam farther out, and another built elaborate sandcastles on the beach. Men played cricket and women gathered with the smaller children. Voices swirled into streams of laughter and shouts. The sun was nearly high, almost noon, time for lunch.

My mother unfolded the tablecloth and spread it on a blanket. Aunty Min unpacked the breads, cheeses, cold cuts and salads. I opened up a thermos of tea and bottles of water and beer. A call went up: "Lunch, come on, everyone. Lunch."

Eagerly, folk gathered around, towelled off, and settled down to eat. As they tucked in, the noise level subsided. It would drop even further after lunch when the same folk would nap or read the newspaper.

"Where's Ian?" The air went still as my father leapt up and yelled again, "Where's Ian?"

Everyone glanced around hurriedly. Uncle Dick

jumped up and ran after my father to the water's edge. They scanned the horizon but saw nothing, so Daddy dashed back to his bag, grabbed his binoculars and sped down to the water. He panned around, searching for Ian's dark hair—still nothing.

"Get a boat, get one of those paddleboats," he yelled to my uncle as he ran back up the beach and started climbing the rocks. The rest of us sat very quietly watching the men.

"He'll find him, Glad. Don't worry," my aunt said as she leant over and patted Mummy's shoulder. My mother had grown pale and her eyes were filled with tears. This time there was nothing she could do but watch.

Daddy's progress was slow and measured as he climbed the rock-face. He looked smaller and smaller as he made his way up. Scared now for both Ian and Daddy, we waited.

"Out there, out there," my father yelled from high up the rocks. "I see him way out there." Daddy scrambled and leapt back down and tore across the sand to the boat. He jumped in, along with my uncle, and they started to paddle furiously. Eventually, they were so far out we couldn't see them. My mother stared into the distance as though she could will them back.

At least half an hour passed before the boat came back into sight. Still we sat quiet. Had Daddy found Ian? Was he all right? Some of our family got up and walked to the water's edge to see better. Mother stayed put, silent.

"They've got him. Look, he's hanging onto the back of the boat." Cries of joy went up and I ran over to hug Mummy. "He's okay Mummy. Ian's okay." She smiled gently and sighed with relief.

As the boat made shore, my brother ran up to our family encampment. He shook the water from his hair and said, "Sorry Mum. I just wanted to see how far out I could go."

"You what?" yelled my father, as he ran back from the boat. "You bloody well what?"

"I just wanted to see how strong I am."

"I told you not to go out too far, not to go out of sight." As he screamed, Daddy smacked Ian across his face. Ian staggered and bent over. We all fell silent. Ian was sixteen, too old to be reproved like that in public. As he stood up, he nursed the red side of his face with one hand and looked hard at Daddy. Suddenly, his fist shot out and landed on his father's chin. Daddy sank to his knees.

NOTHING WRONG

The classroom was downright stuffy. Thirty-four of us sat in our summer uniform, shirtwaist dresses in pale blue, yellow, green or pink, white socks and brown shoes. The room was silent except for pens scratching paper, nibs clattering against the side of inkwells, papers rustling as they were turned, and an occasional sigh. This was the summer of 1957 and, for us thirteen year-olds, the French final exam. Now was the moment of truth: we either knew the answers, or we didn't.

I sat there sweating, anxious. I didn't have the answers, I knew I didn't! No matter how hard I studied, I just didn't remember the work. I thought of all the time I'd spent with a private tutor, extra hours on Saturdays when other kids were out playing. I couldn't answer the questions, I couldn't concentrate, but I couldn't fail. When Mother read my report card each term, she'd purse her lips and shake her head as she muttered, "Not good enough. Just not good."

Dad would read my card and try not to grin. When he tucked me in at bedtime, as he did every night, he would say something like, "Your mother's pretty upset at your report card," but then he'd smile and hug me and tell me not to worry.

I slid my textbook out from under the desk and balanced it on my knees. I checked that the teacher was deep into her book. I flipped the pages and ran my eyes quickly down the verbs. *Je suis, tu es, il est, nous sommes, vous êtes, ils sont.* Stealthily, I returned the book and started the section that dealt with correctly conjugating verbs. That much I could fill in now. The other parts I completed in a wild fashion—marks on the paper so it wouldn't be blank. I had a sick, empty feeling in the pit of my stomach. Why wasn't this over? Why was I here, again, in this place where I couldn't get it right?

As the time passed my mind wandered to the previous spring. I had been sitting in the kitchen, eating my breakfast porridge when my father said, "Gill, you're not going to school today. Your mother and I will drop you off at a doctor's office. Actually, he's a psychiatrist. You'll be taking a whole assortment of tests." When I asked why, he explained, "You try hard but don't seem to do very well." He pulled out a chair and sat down next to me. "Last year you got an A in art and trigonometry, and failed all the rest, including algebra. You have to use algebra to solve the trigonometry problems, so we want to understand how you could fail algebra and pass trig." He went on to explain that the tests would not be difficult, and that they'd pick me up later in the day, when I'd finished. The rest of my porridge quickly congealed into a hard, grey lump as I left it untouched.

The day passed quickly and the tests were actually fun. Some were word games, others required drawing, and a few included building with blocks and cards. There seemed to be no wrong answers and I whizzed along.

I was reunited with my parents in the psychiatrist's office at mid-afternoon. Dad gave me a quick hug and Mummy smiled. I knew I had tried hard. The door opened and the doc came in carrying a thick file.

"I want you to know that Gillian worked really hard today and we learnt a lot from her test scores." He settled into his chair behind the big desk and spread the papers out. He ran his eyes up and down them, flipping them over as he went. Then he leant back in his chair and looked at them again. "There appears to be nothing wrong with your daughter. She scores high on all the appropriate age-related tests, even very high on some of them. She's very bright and grasps concepts easily."

My chest swelled. I was so proud. Dad pulled me over and gave me another hug. Mother nodded her approval. I looked around expectantly. What now?

"So, maybe Gillian could wait outside for a few minutes?"

Dad nodded and I made my way out.

Less than a minute later, my Mother came out of the office, walked past me and down the corridor. Dad followed close behind, grabbing my hand as he went. We got to the car and I saw Mummy standing there, white-lipped, her eyes flashing, furious. We climbed into the car and had a tense and silent ride home.

Later that evening, I overheard Mother on the phone with her sister, Aunty Min.

"Yes, yes. He said Gillian's just fine. But I had to leave when he suggested Brian and I talk about our marriage, and you know why I can't do that." I was confused. I thought this whole day had been about helping me, not about them.

The recess bell rang, pulling my mind away from that day and back into the classroom and the exam that sat before me. It was over now. An excited gaggle of voices broke out as we poured out of the room and flew down the corridor. In the playground, we ran around yelling and letting off steam. It felt good.

And then I saw a prefect waving me over, holding a yellow slip of paper. "Gillian, Miss Pearse wants to see you. Go to her room."

I sighed. It seemed like I was always in the queue outside the headmistress's office waiting to be reprimanded for my latest prank. I walked back through the old buildings and sat on one of the metal chairs. I was third in line. Eventually, I found myself standing in front of her.

"Gillian, I have been told that you were seen cheating in the French exam this afternoon. Is this true?"

My shoulders slumped and I nodded my head.

"I want you to do two things for me. You will retake the exam next week with no books to help. You will also go home today and tell your parents that you were seen cheating. That's all. You may go now."

I crept out of her office, collected my jacket and satchel and rode home on the bus. I chose a seat away from my friends. I stared out the window and tried to imagine telling Dad. Telling Mum didn't matter so much, because I always made her mad. I'd become used to that. But telling Dad, that was a scary thought. He was so proud of me and loved me easily, and I knew I'd let him down.

Once home, I joined Mother in the kitchen and helped her unpack groceries and start laying out food for supper. Dad put the car in the garage, came indoors and hung up his jacket. Turning towards me, he said, "Gill, I got a call from Miss Pearse this afternoon."

I stopped slicing the bread and just stood there. My mouth was dry and my hands trembled.

"Do you have something to tell me?"

I nodded my head.

"Well, what? Look at me when I talk to you."

I was silent. Tears filled my eyes. I couldn't look up. "She said I had to tell you I cheated on the French exam."

"Yes, that's what she told me. Did you?"

When I finally I looked, I saw that his face was hard and his eyes steely blue. I nodded again.

The quiet was broken when my father lunged across the kitchen table and swung wildly, slapping me hard across my face. The bread knife flew out of my hand and clattered onto the floor.

"How dare you?" he bellowed. "How dare you shame me? Go to your room right now."

I ran out the door, scrambled up the stairs and fled to my bedroom. I curled up under the eiderdown, my face stinging and my ears ringing. I sobbed quietly. No protector left; no one to know how desperately I had tried. I remembered the psychiatrist; I knew I wasn't stupid. There was no call for supper.

The next morning I got up, went downstairs, ate breakfast and took the bus to school. Nothing more was said.

I retook the exam...and failed.

CROSSROADS

I rode my motorcycle across London and the roads were slick from last night's rain. I was torn between driving safely and hurrying to make my 8:00 a.m. curfew. At this hour, everything was shrouded in a gray mist and the road was quite empty. It was Saturday and most folk were lingering with their morning tea and newspaper. I peered through the mist and hoped the rain would hold off until I was safely home.

I sat at the red traffic light at the crossroads on Blackheath Common. To my left, the green heathland spread away into the distance. On the corner to my right was an old English pub with black beams, white stucco, and a carriage entrance that led to an inner courtyard. A couple of cars, probably left the previous night by owners unfit to drive, sat in the parking lot next to the pub. Abruptly, the noise of cars braking and engines accelerating snapped my eyes back to the traffic light. As it turned from orange to green I pulled in the clutch, dropped the gear pedal into first and opened the throttle. My motorcycle took off with all the speed and noisy enthusiasm that its 175 cc engine could muster. Curfew time was closing in.

This curfew was based on an understanding I'd reached with my father. Although I was eighteen, he felt that some kind of parental supervision was still appropriate. The agreements we had were often more to do with pacifying or avoiding altercations with my mother than with his need to supervise my young adult life. And so we had reached the understanding that I could stay overnight with my friends on Friday or Saturday, providing I was back in the house before eight the next morning. For my father's part, he would rumple my bedding so it looked like I had just got out of bed. Should my mother rise before eight and look for me, he would say that I had gone out. If she rose after eight, I was in my room. And so the two of us colluded in giving me the freedom I sought, in deceiving my mother and in allowing my father to maintain control.

In my family, there was a history of excluding my mother, made possible by her profound deafness. For most of my childhood, I experienced two simultaneous conversations being carried on in our home: one was loud and laborious and included all four of us; the other was sotto voce and intended only for my father, my brother, and myself.

I rode through London's outer suburbs to my home, where I parked my motorcycle in the back garden, shed my leather jacket, boots and crash helmet, and walked quietly to my room. I lit the gas fire and slurped down the half-cold cup of tea my father had left at my bedside before he went off to the Saturday morning meeting of his amateur radio club. Later, I went down to the kitchen, fixed my own breakfast, and decided that the inclement weather made it a good day to tune up my motorcycle. I retreated to the garage and spent three or four hours wiping, polishing, oiling and generally working on the bike. At lunchtime, I joined my mother and father in the kitchen, where we ate and chatted. Weekend afternoons at our house were usually quiet now that Ian was grown and gone.

Somewhere around six that evening my mother called us in for supper, an informal meal of cold cuts, cheeses, breads and scones, and we helped ourselves. I normally watched the evening news with my parents, and often a play or film, but on this particular evening my mother announced that she was going to bed early because of a headache. My father and I sat in the living room and watched my favourite Wild West program, Champion, the Wonder Horse. A while later, he poured himself a scotch, a liberal one with not too much water, and started to talk. On such an evening we would often spend an hour or so talking about school, or work, or just the world.

"Gill, I want to explain what you saw when you were riding home this morning. I know that while you were sitting at the red light at Blackheath crossroads you looked over into the pub parking lot."

Damn, how did he know where I was early this morning? What else did he know of my whereabouts? I sat still and listened. Despite the open fire burning in the grate, I felt myself getting chilled.

"You looked directly into my car. You saw me

sitting there with a woman. Then you focused back on the road and drove off."

As he spoke, he swilled his scotch around his glass and eyed it contemplatively. He took a sip and looked at me over the rim of his glass. I began to understand: he believed that I had seen him, that we had seen and recognized each other.

"Yes, I did stop at the lights on Blackheath," I confirmed with a nod.

"You know that your mother and I don't see eye to eye on many things," he said, staring into his drink. "Sometimes our relationship has been rocky, which has made things stressful and difficult." I wasn't sure where this was going, but my hands went clammy and cold. I was scared.

"On many occasions your mother has been unresponsive to me. I think you know what I mean." I knew exactly what he meant, and I didn't want to know anymore. "So, at times, I've had friendships that mother doesn't know about. What you saw this morning," he added, keeping his eyes averted, "was me with my lover."

I looked at him as though from afar and saw a tall, slender, blonde, handsome man with a winsome smile and charming ways. I tried to integrate this new information with my perception of my Daddy. He was cuddly, funny, smart and solid. He adored me from the moment I was born and looked out for me all the time. And now he was shattering my world. I said nothing. There was a long silence.

"This relationship is very important to me," he admitted. "In fact, it's what enables me to stay with your mother. I need you to know that if you tell her what you saw, our family will probably break apart. I need you to keep what you saw between us."

Another crossroad. If I kept my father's confidence, life would stay much as it was; if I told my mother, it was very possible that our lives would become vastly different from what they now were. The one person I would have looked to for guidance was the man asking me to remain silent.

I wish I could say that, at that time, I had the strength of character and maturity of conviction to tell my father that I could not betray my mother. But I didn't. Instead, I sat silently as he crossed the room to pour himself another scotch. As he turned, he handed one to me. He had never before offered me a hard drink. I took it, and together we watched the nine o'clock news and chatted about the day's football results.

LIKE THAT

The early evening fog was patchy as I rode my motorcycle across London. I wanted to reach my parents' home before they did, but I was cutting it close. Daddy had asked me to be there when he brought Mummy home from the hospital.

I turned into their driveway and pulled my bike into the garage. I let myself into the house, stoked the boiler and turned up the heat. The small fire I lit in the living room fireplace removed the autumn chill. In the kitchen, I laid out a tray for afternoon tea and found the biscuit tin. With everything done, I felt a sense of relief, knowing these touches would welcome my parents home.

Six weeks earlier, my mother had undergone elective surgery to improve her hearing. For years she'd strained to hear the world around her. She'd worn a hearing aid—one of the old-fashioned, clunky ones with an earpiece and wires that ran down to a huge battery pack tied around her waist. She'd always hated it, but she hated being excluded even more. When she received a letter from her hearing consultant explaining a new surgical procedure that might help her, she grabbed at the chance. Her marriage had been severely affected by her hearing loss and she was willing to take a risk.

When she awoke from the anaesthetic, nurses and family were delighted that she could hear much better. In fact, she had regained sixty percent of her hearing and I didn't need to shout anymore. A few days later, a major problem developed: a nerve that ran down the side of her face had collapsed, paralysing the right side. This caused her eye to squint and weep, her mouth to drag down on one side and her speech to slur. She looked as though she'd suffered a stroke. When I looked at her damaged face, I wanted to curl up and cry. She was rushed back into surgery, where attempts were made to repair the nerve, but success was minimal. Doctors told her the nerve might get stronger with time, but there was nothing more they could do. She had to accept that the trade-off for improved hearing was facial disfigurement.

I heard the key in the front door and ran to open it. Mother stood there alone. "Brian's parking the car."

"Fine, come on in Mummy," I said as I hung up her coat, and led her into the living room. I settled her in her favourite chair and went back to the kitchen to brew the tea. As it steeped, I dashed into the bathroom to use the toilet, and then raced back for the tray, which I carried into the room. My mother looked at me with horror. Her voice shook when she asked, "What's that? Gill, what's that awful noise?"

I looked around in bewilderment. "What noise?"

"It sounds like water flooding."

It took a moment for me to understand. "Mummy, that's just the toilet cistern flushing and refilling!" We both laughed as I gave her a quick hug.

I wondered what was taking Dad so long. I set the tray down and ran out to the garage where he was hunched over his work bench, swearing as he whacked something with a hammer. I told him tea was ready, but he continued hammering. When I asked him to join us inside, he said, "I can't. I can't look at her like that."

"Come on," I urged him. "She's waiting."

I walked back into the house and poured tea. Mummy and I chatted.

Dad didn't come in.

YOURS

Black and clunky, our first telephone sat on a low, round coffee table next to the settee in the living room. All angles, with a white and chrome dial, it held centre place. Nearby, its quiet companions were a notebook containing important names and numbers, and a notepad and pencil.

Neither I nor my brother touched it, only adults got to use it. If it rang and they weren't around, we ran to tell them, or just let it ring, we didn't answer it. Somewhere along the way, it was replaced with a newer model with softer angles and a smaller dial.

But that's the way it stayed, adults only, until long after I left home at eighteen. On return visits, I still called my parents when it rang, I only answered at their behest.

On this particular day, I changed, I crossed an unknown bridge: the phone rang and I answered, "Eltham 7010."

In England, it was the custom to answer by stating the phone number. I listened to a woman's voice, expecting her to ask for one of my parents. What I heard was, "I hate calling you at home but I can't meet you at six. I can't get there until seven at the earliest...."

As she spoke, I realised that she thought she was talking to my father, we did sound alike, so I interrupted with, "I think you want to talk with my father." I dropped the receiver onto the table, sprinted up the stairs to my dad's radio room and cracked the door.

He looked up and I tossed him the word, "Yours."

He and I never spoke of this, but we both knew I'd run into one more of his girlfriends. I kept his secret safe, but I never answered their phone again.

HIS CHILD

It was September, 1964, and I was turning twenty-one. Very adult. The age of legal adulthood. The right to marry, to vote, to own property, to buy alcohol and cigarettes. The age of responsibility. I was very excited.

My girlfriend, June, and I were busy planning my celebrations. My grand treat was to be a weekend in Paris, roaming the Champs Elysees, eating in sidewalk cafes and dancing through the night. But events of a more traditional nature were also arranged.

A train ride into Kent took June and me to my family home. Here, friends and relatives gathered for afternoon tea bringing gifts and good wishes. I was especially proud of the silver coffee percolator my parents gave me – I'd lusted after one for some time. And we'd arranged a party at our flat in the centre of London. My parents generously provided the cake and the drinks for the event.

Mummy and Daddy also agreed to drive up to town and take June and me to dinner. This was a huge concession, as my father hated driving into inner London. Just as they arrived, there was another ring of the door bell and a huge bouquet of red roses—twenty-one exactly—arrived. They were fresh with water glistening on the petals and a rich, heady scent. Mummy admired them and told me to arrange them carefully in a vase and then I stood them near my gifts, coffee pot included, and my cake. This was the first time my parents had visited our flat and we were proud to show off our home. It was small, but it was sufficient and located just around the corner from Marble Arch.

Dinner was a great success. We'd all dressed up for the occasion, even I'd worn a dress and had my hair done. The Italian restaurant was festive, the food good, Mummy was relaxed and the chatter was easy. Daddy entertained with stories and June was witty and bright. At evening's end I was sorry to see my parents go.

Back in our flat, June and I tidied up and chatted about the evening. I took out the card that came with the flowers and read aloud.

"Congratulations.

Love, Brian & Rosalind.

Don't forget dinner on Wednesday."

We marvelled at the synchronicity of both people and flowers, and the audacity of my father in sending the bouquet from him and his lover.

The following Wednesday, June and I returned to the same restaurant, where the atmosphere was still festive and the food good. But the woman greeting me, hugging me, congratulating me, was not my mother. Rosalind was younger, more vivacious and far more glamorous. I looked at Daddy's smile, his sparkling eyes and I could see he was in love. Conversation flew back and forth, along with lots of laughter and June came into her own as she found an audience for her slightly risqué repartee. When coffee was served, my father left the table to take care of the bill. Rosalind turned to me, reached across the table and took my hand. "I want you to know your father is a wonderful man and I love him dearly."

I looked at her and said, "I know."

And then I drained my wine glass.

"I just want to have his child so desperately."

"I understand," I responded as I withdrew my hand. At the same time, I was thinking, Who the hell does she think I am? I am his child!

NOT THE CASE

It was Sunday afternoon and Antonia, my new girlfriend, and I were visiting my parents for afternoon tea. The dining room was full of relatives and friends. Mother and I were busy, back and forth to the kitchen, keeping the sandwich and cake plates filled and the teapot topped up. I always chuckled when I found myself doing this. Here I was at twenty-five, still working alongside mother to serve afternoon tea. She'd taught me how to help when I was about eight, and it had become Gill's job.

Antonia was busy recounting tales of our latest camping trip. Folk enjoyed listening to her, as she turned the mundane into something quite funny. I watched her, and looked around at the faces, and recognized how fortunate I was that no-one ever questioned why I brought a particular friend home. They never asked what happened to old friends or where I met new ones. They just welcomed them with a hug and offered tea.

I heard the telephone ringing in the living room. Daddy slid through the dining room door, the echo of his quick footsteps fading as he went down the hallway. Almost immediately, he reappeared in the doorway and nodded at me, so I joined him in the hallway.

"It's June," he told me.

"I don't want to talk to her."

"Why not?"

"I just don't. Tell her I'm not here….anything…. but I won't talk with her."

He gave me a long, hard look as he turned away. I knew I was in trouble.

I rejoined everyone in the dining room and chatted cheerfully as I tried to work out how to sidle out of the house without facing my father. By late afternoon, most of the guests had left and Antonia and I were helping Mother clear up. As I made one last run to the dining room, my father stopped me in the hallway.

"Gill, June has been a guest in this house for four or five years. Why won't you talk to her?"

"I just don't want to," I told him.

He stood very still and narrowed his eyes, as though he were considering his words carefully. Finally, he asked, "Was this a lesbian relationship?"

Everything became so quiet that I heard nothing but the ringing in my ears. This was uncharted territory. We didn't talk about my affairs, only my father's. All I could do was nod.

"Well, you need to know that I don't care whether your lovers are male or female. I only care that you handle them respectfully, like a Herbert. Now get in there and call June, while I go talk with your mother."

I slunk into the living room and called June. Luckily, she must have gone out because there was no reply. As I walked back down the hallway to the dining room, I braced myself for my mother's words. She was sitting in her overstuffed armchair; she didn't move. I was quaking. She smiled and held out her hands. I reached over and took them.

"I'm so glad to finally know," she told me. She went on to say she always knew I was different and she worried all the time. "I thought maybe you were into drugs or alcohol," she said. "I'm just so glad that's not the case."

LIKE GILL

The droning phone drilled into my sleep. I rolled over and buried my head under my pillow. It was ruthless in its persistence. Damn. Unplugging the phone or turning off the ringer weren't options back then, so before falling asleep I'd used several cushions to bury the red plastic base and cord. For good measure, I'd stuffed it all into a cupboard. It was Sunday morning and I really wanted to sleep in. But Sunday morning was when my mother wanted me up and chatting with her. She wasn't going away.

I stumbled into the living room and dug the cushions out of the cupboard. I grabbed the handset and answered.

"There you are! I'm so glad I caught you because your father and I are going for afternoon tea to The Castle Hotel in Eynsford, and I wanted to know if you and Antonia wanted to come too."

I scrunched up my face and rubbed my eyes to block out the bright light. "Mummy, I've told you not to call so early. It's eight o'clock and we've no idea what we're doing today."

"Don't be so silly. You should be up by now, it's a beautiful day."

No day was beautiful if it was earlier than ten! "No, we're not coming for tea. Enjoy yourselves, bye."

I slunk back to bed and curled up next to Antonia.

By early afternoon we decided that afternoon tea did sound like a good idea. It was too late to call and accept the invitation, and we knew better than to show up late. We leapt into the shower and dressed in 'something decent'—meaning no blue jeans. Gray slacks, crisp blue shirt, cravat and tweed hacking jacket would do for me.

Some speedy driving took us across town and out through the lush green fields of Kent. We drove down country lanes with high hedgerows, past small villages with folk gathered on the greens, and into Eynsford, where we parked and ran up the hotel steps. It was four fifteen, meaning we were both unexpected and late!

I explained to the hostess that we were joining my parents, who I could see at a table by the window overlooking the beautiful gardens. As we waited for the couple in front of us to be seated, my father looked directly at me but showed no sign of recognition. What the hell had I done now, what secret had I unwittingly betrayed? Whatever it was, I didn't want to deal with it. The hostess said, "This way, please," and we threaded our way through the sea of tables. As we got close to my parents' table, my father looked up, appeared somewhat startled, and then smiled broadly and greeted us with warm hugs. As he let me go, he said, "I looked across the room and thought how much that young man looked like my Gill."

I sank into the chair. My own father had seen

what I wanted the world to see—a young man—but he hadn't recognised his own daughter.

ON HIM

The Brass Bell stood prominently on the street corner with lights blazing, sign swaying and music blaring out of its windows. People streamed in and out, their laughter drifting over to us as we edged our car into the kerb.

The oldest pub in the neighbourhood, it featured two separate entrances. One door was marked "Public Bar" and was where tradesmen in jeans and boots stopped for a pint on their way home, or brought their wives later in the evening for a game of darts and friendly banter with their mates. The other door read "Saloon Bar" and was where dark-suited city workers just off their commuter trains gathered to mull over the day's economic news, or brought their girlfriends for a quick drink before dinner or the theatre.

From experience, we knew we'd get less reaction if we used the Public Bar. Antonia's mini dress and my slacks and shirt were giveaways, and some smart-mouthed chap might throw a remark about "two birds needing a real guy." But that was rare. In the Saloon Bar we knew from experience we'd receive frosty looks and a show of backs. Those close to the bar would have fallen silent and turned away as I approached to order drinks.

The long bar served both rooms. It ran across the middle of the space and separated these two very different worlds. I nodded at a couple of local lads I'd played darts with and found us a table in the corner. Once Antonia was seated, I manoeuvred my way to the bar, where I ordered a scotch with water, no ice, and a glass of chardonnay.

As I waited for the bartender, I looked over into the Saloon. From the other side, a group's loud, teasing voices and laughter floated over, the conversation focused on tearing apart the previous evening's football games.

As I listened, I noticed a couple at the other end of the bar. They stood together, nursing their drinks, voices low and faces earnest. Oblivious to the noise around them, they saw only each other. She was small, about five feet, and of slight build. Her hair was dark and curly; when she looked up, I saw she was very pretty. Her partner stood six-feet, and had blonde hair. He was handsome, his features familiar. He had a charming smile and stood with one arm protectively around her shoulder. I'd never seen her before.

Suddenly, the bartender was placing our drinks in front of me, "That'll be five and six, please," he said.

"Tell that man at the end of the bar that the drinks are on him," I replied.

The bartender walked over, leant towards the man and, pointing to me, said, "She says her drinks are on you."

The man looked at me. I raised my glass before turning my back on my father.

ACT III:

CURTAIN CALL

A SHIFTING SHADOW

We had just finished lunch. As my father and I chatted, his eyelids began to flutter, he shifted in his chair, looked directly at me and tried to follow my words. But, inevitably, his eyes gently closed and he began to snore lightly. I watched his chest gently rise and fall, the man stretched out in his favourite armchair in the living room. As he grew older, these after-lunch naps had become a necessity.

My visits with my parents were very special for all of us, but it was hard to make them work logistically. I flew from California to London not more than every two years, so we wanted our visits to last for more than a few hours. But in truth, as my parents aged into their late seventies, a few hours was all they could handle. Knowing this, I tried to visit them at least two or three times while I was in London.

I watched my father and realized just how old and frail he had become. When he was awake, I saw and felt the father that I had always known: enthusiastic, charming, athletic, handsome, competent, capable and very much in control. As he slept however, I saw a shadow of the man he once was. His thinning hair, double chin, rounded belly, his gnarled hands, none of the features that came to mind when thinking about him, but what I saw as he slept.

Leaving my father to rest, I quietly joined my

mother in her bedroom. Seated next to her bed, we chatted through her afternoon rest. I told her how, when my father picked me up at the railway station, he had called me Julian. And he did the same thing again just before he fell asleep. "Each time I corrected him," I explained, "and each time he was flustered by his error. Has he been having memory problems or confusion?"

My mother explained that his memory had become poor, and that he got very irritable. "I've tried giving him a list of chores or groceries to buy when he goes out," she said, "but often that doesn't work. He forgets he has a list, so he goes to the stores he knows well, like the bakery, and buys whatever he recognizes."

I took her hand. "How frustrating, especially as you don't drive." I thought of all the times I'd simply leapt into my car and run out on a quick errand.

"I can't tell you how many times he brings home food we don't need or like, or library books I've already read. I get scared." She looked away before adding, "How long will it be before he gets lost and doesn't come home?"

My mother went on to describe a recent visit of old friends, and how my father had monopolized the conversation with war stories. She wished he would talk more of current events, or even of stories that related to our family as a whole. "I want him to focus on our lives and the adventures we had together."

As I sat with her, I realized that she might be

feeling that painful loneliness that strikes when a loved one fails to recognize a life partner. "Do you miss him?" I asked. "Are you lonely?"

She responded with that slow quiet smile I knew so well and said, "No, he's still with me, but I fear the future."

I swept her into a bear hug and caressed her hair. She held still for a while and then sat back and declared, "I think it's time for a cup of tea." With that, she stood and walked to the kitchen.

The clatter of cups and saucers told me she was laying the tea tray. Running water splashed into the kettle and the biscuit tin lid clanged as she took out ginger snaps and digestive biscuits.

I returned to the living room and gently touched my father's arm. "Daddy," I said quietly, my voice nudging him awake. "Have you been forgetting things?"

He sat up in his chair and stared at me. After a moment he said matter-of-factly, "I do get a bit confused sometimes, but it's okay. I know what's going on, that I've had several small strokes. That's the cause of the memory loss."

I strove to keep my face calm as I listened, not moving, as I grappled for a response. "Have you told your doctor?"

"There's not much point, as there's nothing he can do. And it would only upset your mother."

I recognized the truth of his words, and his decision not to talk about his health. This was a stoic man who had always accepted the inevitable. I settled onto the couch and smiled at him. I wanted him to know that it was okay with me. It was all okay. But I knew not to discuss his decision. He needed me to respect it. After a time, I leant over and hugged him. I was struck by how fragile he had become, with his skin papery dry. As we held one another, his hands grasping me, the image I'd always held of my father began to shift in my mind. Now, he was an old man.

SOTTO VOCE

As the plane dropped for its final approach the scenery turned to a blur and I recalled my seven-year-old self gazing out at these same fields. That time we were leaving England and returning to Egypt after a summer holiday back home. I remember the foggy patch that had grown on the window as I peered out at green fields. I turned to my father and said, "Dad, I still don't know why Mummy isn't coming with us."

He ruffled my hair. "Remember how hard it's been for Mummy to hear you lately?"

My face fell as I nodded.

"She's staying for an operation so she can hear you again. She'll be back soon. Don't worry."

My older brother seemed to agree, and I knew that if he believed it, so could I.

I snuggled close to Dad as the drone of the plane lulled me into a quiet doze.

None of us had dreamt Mother's surgery would worsen her hearing, but it did. Our family, already split along mother-and-son, father-and-daughter lines, now became even more fractured between the hearing and the deaf. Dad had taught us to run two conversations simultaneously: one was slow and ponderous, and included Mother: the other fast, light and just for the hearing.

Ten years later, at eighteen, I walked into the

living room and joined my parents who were seated around the fire. As we watched the end of the news, I said quietly to my father, "Dad, I went to the RAF enlistment office today."

He didn't turn to look at me, but asked, "Why?"

"I can join as an officer, because I aced my hotel and restaurant program, but I'm under twenty-one, so I need you to sign the papers."

"No way," he responded. "No daughter of mine is going into the Air Force. That's it! And don't bother your mother with this—it's not happening."

We all continued to stare at the TV. No more was said and my mother was unaware that my dream had just been smashed.

Many years later, as I sat chatting with my mother about my career, she said, "Gill, I always wondered why you never wanted to be in the services. I thought you'd do really well in the RAF – but you never showed any interest."

I felt anger welling up as I explained that I had wanted to enlist, but Dad had refused to sign the papers.

I saw sadness in her face as she spoke. "I wonder why. He loved his time in the service." And then she paused before saying, "Why didn't you ask me? I'd have signed them."

For a brief moment, I hated my father.

Later, in my early forties, I took my partner to meet my parents. My father welcomed us at the front door and, beneath the loud, warm greetings, he delivered an undercurrent of comments about my mother. It didn't register with me, any more than it registered during the other moments that day held when quiet, hidden conversations occurred, conversations that excluded my mother. That evening, as my partner and I rode the train back across London, she asked me why we shut my mother out. I could only reply that this is what my father had created, and we had followed suit. Her puzzled, questioning look took me aback, and I began to ask myself why we did this. I considered how little I knew or trusted my mother, and suddenly understood that Dad was responsible. He'd hijacked me for his companion. For thirty two years, I had participated.

The plane dropped onto the runway, I picked up a rental car and drove to my parents' home.

Stacking my suitcases in the hallway, I walked into the living room. Dad got up and gave me a welcoming hug. I walked over and bent down to my mother. Hugging her gently, I heard my father ask quietly,

"How was the trip?"

I turned to my mother, looking her full in the face. "Daddy just asked me about my plane trip."

Out of the corner of my eye I saw Dad stiffen, his face tighten, his eyes narrow. He glared at me. I looked back at mother.

"It was long and boring, but I'm glad to see you."

Now I understood the damage my father had created with 'sotto voce'. That day, I killed it.

UPPER HAND

The train swayed and rumbled as it travelled through London and into Kent. Smoky-gray buildings gave way to snatches of green fields with hedgerows and the occasional cow. My mind drifted back to the last time I'd made this familiar trip. Daddy had met me at the station and we'd driven to my parents' home through the rural villages and country lanes. At one point he'd pointed out a row house and remarked, "I was billeted there during WWII while I served on the nearby air base at Biggin Hill. I really liked the woman who lived there. She had a great laugh. Her husband was off fighting somewhere in France."

He paused slightly. I waited.

"I heard she had a baby the following year, a girl. I often wondered what her husband made of that!"

I said nothing and continued to gaze out the front window. Was this yet another of Dad's flings? Did I have a stepsister?

The train jerked me back as it pulled into the station. From the window, I could see Daddy pacing to and fro on the platform, pushing his glasses up his nose as he peered around. At eighty, his back was much more stooped.

I jumped down just as the train shuddered to a stop and ran over to him. We hugged and then turned and walked towards his car. As we climbed in he said, "Gill, I've got to talk to you. Now."

His tone was serious and his voice cracked slightly. Sweat lined his upper lip and he fiddled with his keys.

"Okay, Dad, let's talk."

"She knows, Gill. Your mother knows everything."

"Knows what?"

"About all the women."

His voice broke and a lone tear slid down his cheek. "She's got me cornered now because she knows." I asked him to explain and he said, "Ian and his girlfriend, Eve, were visiting, and Eve and I were bantering and teasing each other. I made a risqué comment and she lost her temper. In her rage she turned to your mother and screamed, 'Gladys, you really should know how unfaithful Brian has been. He's always had girlfriends on the side.' Your mother was very quiet but responded, 'I think you'd better leave now.' As we all moved into the hallway, Eve was still yelling and I was shouting back. At the door, Eve turned, picked up the potted plant that was on the shelf, and threw it at me. Ian grabbed her and dragged her out the door. So, you see, she knows, your mother knows."

"What did she say, Daddy?"

"I asked her if she wanted me to leave. She looked surprised and told me she had always known, so there was no reason for me to go anywhere. And then she said it was time for a cup of tea."

"I'm so sorry, Daddy."

"And now, I have to do whatever she asks. She's got the upper hand. I'm a broken man."

I looked across at the old man my father had become. I heard the humiliation in his voice. For over fifty years he'd taken pride in his dalliances and deception. Now, he could only suffer Mummy's forgiveness.

TOO LATE

"Gill, Gill, can you hear me?"

I held the phone close as I listened to the slow, measured voice of my cousin Alan who lived in Florida. I hadn't spoken to him for at least twenty years.

"Yes, I'm here."

"Gill, I'm calling from your parents' house. I'd promised to visit them the next time I was in England, and I took the train down here today." Why was he calling me? What had happened? Before I could ask, he said, "Your mother wanted me to call to tell you that your father died this morning. I'm sorry."

My hand grew clammy around the phone and I sank to my knees. "Is she there? Can I speak to her?"

I slid onto my butt and brought my knees up to my chin. Huddled against the wall, I listened to shuffling noises as Alan handed the phone to my mother.

"Gill, I'm so sorry," she told me.

"Mummy, what happened?"

"It was all so quick, but I should have called you before."

"Before what?"

In a frail, quaking voice she explained that Daddy had suffered his first major stroke four days earlier.

"He was in his radio den, talking on the air, with ham radio friends. The phone rang in the main house and it was one of those friends suggesting I check on him. He'd stopped responding to their calls. I opened the door and found him slumped over his desk. The ambulance rushed him to hospital. The doctors said he was doing well and would probably stay only a few days. I decided not to call you until he was back home."

"Why, Mummy? Why didn't you tell me?"

"I knew you'd be on a plane the next day and I wanted you to come when you could help me care for him."

"And?"

"And this morning he stepped out of bed, had another major stroke and died. Now it's too late. I'm sorry."

Too late for me to see him again. "Where's Ian?" I asked. If my brother was there, he could help support Mummy.

"I spoke to him on Friday. He and Eve were leaving for a trip to Sweden. He said he knew you'd come to take care of Dad, so they were going ahead with their trip. He didn't leave any way for me to contact him."

I knew my father would expect me to step up and care for Mummy. He knew she and I were not close, but he also knew that I wouldn't let him down. It was not too late for me to stand in his stead. I told her I'd be on the next plane.

THE GAP

I drove out of Heathrow and turned southeast. Dusk was approaching and there was a slight mist. It was unusually muggy, which left me sweaty and grubby. The flight from San Francisco had been uneventful. My "special circumstances" meant I'd been seated upstairs in business class. But this was the one time I couldn't enjoy the extra legroom or the attentive flight steward. Instead, I'd sat for ten hours with the same words swirling around my mind: "Daddy's dead." I'd plugged in the earphones and let the classical music spill over me and block out the world. My grief locked me in mine.

As I pulled onto the main road and joined the heavy traffic flowing around south London, I tried to focus. The road signs all had familiar names but I couldn't quite get my bearings. Circling a roundabout a couple of times, I finally found the right road. I settled back into my seat, adjusted my mirrors and chewed on a mint. My eyes were tired after so many tears and hours travelling, but this was the last stretch.

It seemed impossible that only thirty-six hours earlier I had been working in my kitchen, installing shelving and making so much noise that I'd barely heard the phone ring. Grabbing it hastily, I'd stopped short when I heard that long hollow echo which told me it was a transatlantic call. I never received transatlantic calls. Instead, I was the one who made them.

Something was wrong.

"Gill. Gill, can you hear me?"

I'd listened to my cousin, Alan, tell me my father had died. I'd grabbed my suitcase and passport and called for the first flight back to England.

Gradually, the streets became familiar and my thoughts shifted to arriving at my parents' house, to greeting my mother. She and I had never been close; somehow, we'd never managed to find each other.

I turned the car into my parents' road and coasted gently to a stop outside the house. Turning the engine off, I sat quietly for a minute. The rush and hustle of the trip dropped away. I sat still, knowing once I entered their home, there was no going back, my father's death would become my reality.

I walked up the path towards the lighted porch, put my key in the lock and opened the door. The house was quiet and dark but a light shone from my parents' bedroom. Walking down the hallway, I pushed the door open. Mother rose from her chair and walked across the room to me. I held out my arms and we hugged. She whimpered, "Oh, Gill," and I felt her body sag slightly as she leant on me.

We stood silent for a moment and then she pulled back and said, "You know, I don't really know you, you were always your father's. But I knew you'd come." She hugged me again. "You're my Gill."

My heart knew her words to be true—we really

didn't know each other; father had always stood between us—but, she was my mother. At that moment, with her words, the gap started to close.

OFF LIMITS

Every inch was crammed with gear: gear next to gear, gear in front of gear, gear on top of gear. Wires ran everywhere; not an empty space. I peered into this tiny room, crowded with mounds of radio equipment. A single bed ran along the wall to the left, and on the right wall was a unit of shelves and cupboards. A deep shelf ran across the cupboards at desk height, forming a work surface; below were more cupboards. I looked at this space in disbelief: the clutter was so high I couldn't even see the woodwork. When my parents moved into the house twenty-five years earlier, I had built these units to my father's exact specifications. I'd loaded them into a van, delivered them to their house and assembled them in this room.

A lifetime amateur radio operator, my father had bought, swapped and built his own equipment. Sixty years of radio paraphernalia was crammed into this room. The available wall space was covered with QSL postcards confirming contacts made on the air. All ham radio guys had their own individually designed cards and they prized their collections. Daddy stuck the ones he'd received on his version of a brag wall—with his own bright yellow card front and centre. His call sign, G2WI ran across the top with little pen line drawings of Red Indians running in and out of the characters. Underneath ran 'Gee, Two Wild

Indians'—words I'd heard him use whenever he was on the air.

This was his 'radio shack'—his den, his passion—his world. And, ultimately, the room in which he'd suffered a major stroke. This was a room we were forbidden to enter unless invited.

My mind raced as I surveyed the chaos. Daddy had died only four days earlier and I felt his absence so keenly in this room: without him, it was cold, silent, useless.

From afar, I heard my mother answer the front door bell and welcome the caller.

"Jim, come on in. It's good to see you."

She brought a man into the room. He shook my hand and said, "Hullo, I'm Jim. Brian asked me, should anything happen to him, to come over and empty his radio shack. He asked me to sell the equipment for your mother, and I've brought a truck to get started."

How logical and practical of my father. He knew neither Mummy nor I would know what to do with this stuff. I stood aside and let Jim start to unhook the gear. I rejoined my mother in the living room and we continued to make funeral arrangements.

Daddy's loyal friend toiled away, making several trips to empty the room. At mid-afternoon I took him a cup of tea and asked how he was doing.

"Good, really good," he told me. "I've cleared anything that might have been a problem and I'll get the rest of the gear tomorrow."

I was slightly puzzled because I was unaware of any possible problems, but I didn't question him. I was too tired and grief-stricken to do more than thank him for his help.

That evening, I heard Mummy chatting on the phone. She promised to send me somewhere in the morning, and then hung up. That's when she explained that she'd been talking with a retired school teacher friend, Sheila, who lived nearby. "I didn't know her very well, but your father knew her better. She called to offer her condolences and to invite you over. As a teenager, you two were in the same Sea Ranger crew and she'd like to see you again."

I had no memory of Sheila but saw no harm in humouring my mother.

Next morning, I drove over to Sheila's and introduced myself. She claimed to remember me, although I had no recall of her. We chatted for a while about my father and I wondered casually why I was there. Daddy's death was so very recent and I was devastated, I didn't have much to say to this woman.

Then she said, "You know, your dad would often drop by and visit. We saw each other a lot. I was very fond of him."

As her chatter went on, my mind became very still. These two had been close? I'd never heard of Sheila.

"In fact, we used to write each other poetry. Did you know he was a good poet?"

Now it was my heart that stood still. I had no idea he wrote poetry. I didn't want to be there. She asked if I wanted to hear some of his poems and told me she'd saved them all. She also told me she'd written many poems to him, and that he'd saved them in a box in his radio shack.

I thought of Jim rummaging around in the shack. Daddy knew we wouldn't go in—it was "off limits."

I declined to listen to my father's poems and left as gracefully as I could. As I drove away, I wondered how many more times I'd be stung by my father's infidelity.

NOT MY JOB

As weak sunlight filtered through the curtains, I clutched my pillow and shrank into my mattress. I didn't want this day, the day of my father's funeral.

Ever since I'd arrived from California, time had flown by in a blur of phone calls, financial meetings and mundane household chores, including taking the cat to the vet. So much activity that I'd had little time to grieve my father's death, to miss him. But there was no avoiding it this day.

The funeral procession was scheduled to commence at eleven o'clock; the hearse carrying his body, and the limousines, would come to my parents' house. From there, followed by a line of cars carrying friends and family, we would all proceed to the local church. After the service, there would be another ride to the crematorium, and then back to our house for tea and scones.

I toyed with the sheets and gazed at the ceiling. I played the day's events out in my mind. I thought of all the handshakes and hugs, all the faces, all the expressions of grief. I didn't want to do this. I just wanted to be left alone, to howl in pain and loss.

I heard my mother in the kitchen and then her footsteps coming down the hallway. She stopped outside my room and quietly opened the door. "Here's your tea, Gill."

I looked at her drawn and weary face, and at

the yellow teacup. For forty-eight years my father had brought me tea every morning I'd slept in their house. Now Mummy was picking up where he'd left off.

As she bent over and put down the cup and saucer, I reached up and hugged her. Very softly, she said, "Oh Gill. Today's going to be very hard. I wish Ian was here."

I nodded, still amazed at my brother's decision to go on vacation knowing Daddy had suffered a major stroke. I was appalled he had left no contact information. I could have used his help all week with the mountain of chores. But he wasn't around. Mummy and I would have to do everything ourselves.

By ten-thirty, fragile and shaky, we were both ready to face the day. Stray relatives had been arriving and I'd gathered them into the living room. I was pleased to see my cousins, Alan and Terry. Terry lived nearby and was a quiet, strong man whom Mother trusted. Alan, who lived in Florida, had grown up with my mother sharing his family home before she married. They were very close and his presence was a great comfort to her. We hugged and chatted as we drank coffee and nibbled on biscuits.

The living room door opened once again, and standing in the doorway was the funeral director. His black-tailed suit, bright white shirt and black tie stood in contrast to our muted tones. The time was here. He looked around the room and caught my eye. "It's time to leave," he said. "And I need to know, who is the principal mourner?" He looked around again, pausing as he glanced at the men. I knew about the 'principal mourner' and their duties. Traditionally, this duty went to the eldest male child. From the house to the church, this mourner was to walk behind the hearse as a public expression of grief. The room fell quiet as he waited for a response. This was Ian's job.

I looked at my black loafers, black denim jeans, white shirt and black denim jacket. I looked at the director's dress suit. I took a deep breath and announced, "I am."

As I made my way across the room and out the door, I felt the tension dissipate. Folk began to chat again; the crisis was over.

I walked down the front pathway, turned to the funeral director and asked, "What happens now?"

"Once everyone is ready," he explained, "the hearse will lead the procession to the church. You and I will walk behind the coffin. Are you sure you want to do this?"

Tersely, I muttered, "Yes, I'm sure."

I turned my back to him and the hearse and sat on a low brick wall next to my parents' garden. I looked at their roses; I saw my father's face. I was so angry and he was so calm. Damn Ian. How dare he not be here? It wasn't my job. I wasn't dressed for it; I didn't know how to do it. I was scared. My father continued to smile gently. Just smile at me.

I heard my name called. Slowly I stood, brushed

off my jeans, and walked to the waiting procession. I nodded to the funeral director and stepped into the road next to him. As I lifted my head and gazed straight ahead, I thought, "Okay, Dad, this one's for you."

SO ANGRY

We drove back into the driveway of my parents' house just as dusk fell. The sunshine had disappeared and it was spitting with rain. Mummy and I had spent the day driving through the surrounding countryside and villages. We'd popped into local craft stores and had lunch at the Bo-Peep pub. We'd retraced many of the haunts she and my father had visited. Since his death, Mummy didn't get out much, so the ride was a special treat for both of us.

Mummy navigated her way along the path from the garage to the house, but there she stopped. Steps had become a hazard so she waited for my arm as support. Once inside, we shrugged off our coats and I settled her into her favourite armchair with the day's newspapers. I went to the kitchen, brewed a pot of tea and laid out ginger snaps and chocolate digestive biscuits.

I carried the tray into the living room and poured us each a cup. The tea was warming after the winter chill. As we chatted easily about our day's adventure, I was aware of how safe I felt. Rain was streaming down the windows and beating a tattoo on the roof. This sturdy little bungalow provided comfort and shelter from the outside world, from its clamour and chaos. Sitting with Mummy felt calm and reassuring. So calm and reassuring that I was amazed at the words that tumbled from my mouth. "Mummy, why were you always so angry with me when I was a child?"

She looked at me, eyebrows raised. "Angry? I wasn't angry with you."

"Yes, you were. Every time I came into the room, you looked so angry. I never knew what I'd done wrong. You'd give me a half-hearted smile, but you looked so sad."

Her eyes teared up, and she looked down. The silence was heavy. I waited, hopefully.

"I wasn't angry at you. I was angry with your father—for all his indiscretions. And you looked and sounded just like him. I thought I hid it; I didn't think you knew." She raised her head and held my gaze. "Oh, Gill. I'm so sorry. It wasn't you."

With her words, the hopeless task of trying to please my mother fell from my shoulders. I smiled and nodded, leant over and hugged her. "Makes sense, Mummy, and it's okay."

HER PLAN

My mother looked at me over her teacup. "Gill, do you really think I didn't know?"

I gazed back at her. I was embarrassed. For many years I did think she'd never known. Now I realised how badly I'd underestimated her.

"Let me top up the teapot and then I'll explain what happened." She went to the kitchen and reappeared with the teapot huddled in its cosy. Topping off our cups, she settled back in her chair.

"You see, Gill, I had only been married to your father a couple of years when I found a note in his jacket. I was taking his clothes to the cleaners and had to check that the pockets were empty. I was devastated, but I never said a word to him. I went to Aunty Min and asked her what to do."

Aunty Min was Mummy's older sister and she'd helped raise her after their mother died. She and Mummy were very close and our two families spent a lot of time together.

"We talked for a long time and she told me I had a decision to make. If I wanted to stay married to Brian, I had to figure out how to keep our family together. I had to realise it was up to me. Brian wasn't going to change. He was a charmer, just like his father. So, that's what I did. I did whatever it took to keep him with us."

She smiled her gentle, soft smile.

"You see, it's true that by taking Ian with me to join Brian in Canada during the war I was taking us away from the bombing raids over England. But I also knew that Brian was billeted on the property of a well-known family that had daughters, all of them in their late teens and early twenties. I knew the only way to keep him out of trouble was for me to be there. In fact, at the very first function I attended at the McVies' house, I walked into the living room and found one of the girls sitting really close to Brian on the couch."

"What did you do?"

"I walked over and said, 'I'm sorry, but you're sitting in my seat'."

"What did she do?"

"She got up and left. I sat down. Brian didn't say a word!"

I sipped my tea. I took a deep breath.

"And do you remember the day you came home and told me you'd just learnt that most of your friends' parents shared a bank account? You wanted to know why Brian and I each had separate accounts. At the time, I told you it was because we both worked and it made tracking our money easier. I never told you that the reason I kept teaching all those years was so that I would be financially secure, both in terms of income and in terms of savings, if he did leave."

I let out a sigh. So much I'd seen; so little I'd understood.

"And then there was Egypt."

"What happened in Egypt?"

"Well, it was how we got there, really. You see, you were very ill and we knew you weren't getting better here in England. And I saw Brian getting very restless. I knew that he wanted more than teaching in the suburbs of London. I needed to keep our life challenging and exciting to keep him with us. And then, he showed me this advertisement for teaching posts in Egypt. He was sure I would say no. But I knew it might be just the ticket, so we went. And you did get better."

"Mummy wasn't it very hard for you? Traipsing around the world with two young children!"

"It was. Very hard. I missed Aunty Min and the rest of my family terribly. But I was determined to keep ours together."

I thought back to all the times we'd visited Aunty Min. She baked the best chocolate sandwich cake I've ever eaten and she was always preserving jams and fruit. Her kitchen was warm and welcoming with many taste treats. And I remembered her slightly ironic smile when she talked with my father, as though she was looking at a naughty boy. Now I realised she knew just how naughty!

Slowly I began to understand the price my mother had paid in order to keep our family united. As a child, there had been so many times when I'd wondered why she didn't confront my father, why she didn't stand up to him. Now it was clear that ultimatums were too risky: if forced to make a choice, he might have left. That was to be avoided at all costs.

"So, what happened after we came back from Egypt? Did he settle down?"

"Oh, Gill. I wish. But it became even harder as our lives became more mundane. By this time, you and Ian were both in high school and he was a headmaster. Our routines were very predictable with little excitement, so he just created it for himself. Do you remember the year we had his secretary and her family over for tea at Christmas?"

I remembered it well because I had been surprised and pleased. My best friend back then was Susan and I spent a lot of time at her home. Susan's mother was Daddy's school secretary. My parents did invite Susan along on our vacations so I'd have company, but I thought my mother felt that her family was beneath us and so she didn't socialize with them.

"Well, I knew your father was having an affair with his secretary, and I decided that the best way to let her feel the security of our marriage and our home was to invite her right in! So, I did. They came for afternoon tea and you children went off to play while we adults got to sit together and chat. By the time she left, she'd seen just who she was up against!"

I sat back and grinned. "That was mighty feisty of you to invite her right into the lion's den. I never guessed what was behind it."

"You weren't meant to know. But she and Brian, they knew!"

By now, the light was fading and our tea was cold. I collected the dishes and offered to make a light supper for us. Mother sat back and watched the evening news on the television.

In the kitchen, I washed our teatime dishes, fed her cat and generally tidied up. At eighty-four my mother was still very self-sufficient, but her eyesight was failing and often she just didn't see the dirt! Eventually, I found the fixings and prepared soup and salad for us. I knew it would be easier for her if we ate right there in the living room where she was comfortably ensconced in her chair. I loaded up the trolley and wheeled it in. Together, we ate and watched the end of the news and the weather forecast. I thought a lot about how much I'd misunderstood my mother. Little had I realised that through all the years she had a plan and she'd done whatever she thought would make that plan successful.

"Mummy, why didn't you leave Daddy? Why did you want to stay with him?"

"Gill, you have to remember the times. We're talking about the 1940s, 50s and 60s. If I'd divorced your father I would have automatically gained custody of you and Ian. And you'd have grown up without the father you adored! You wouldn't have liked that. Also, I always loved Brian. He was the only man I wanted."

I nodded. She was right. I'd have been heartbroken to have lost my father.

"And my plan worked. He never left."

AU REVOIR

After my father died my mother continued to live in the bungalow they had shared. They had moved there from the large house when we children were grown and had left home. The bungalow was small and intimate and more than enough for the two of them. It was filled with furniture that had been with them their entire married life.

Here, Mummy was comfortable and comforted. Everything was familiar and known to her. Everything spoke of their fifty years together. For her, my father lived in this house, even though he was no longer there. It was their home, never hers.

When my father died my mother asked me to organize their finances. I'd spent several days working my way through my father's desk and built a detailed picture of their financial life. Then I sat with my mother and we reviewed the bills and bank statements and set up automatic bill payments so she would have less to remember.

Every year, when I flew back to England to visit my mother, we'd review her finances and make any necessary adjustments. Each visit would include spending time with her neighbours, Harry and Ivy. They were her lifeline to the world. They installed an intercom, and they checked on her morning and evening. Ivy brought home her groceries and Harry repaired everything that broke and kept her home safe. Their grown sons would pop over every weekend. Twenty years before, on the day Harry and Ivy moved in, my mother had appeared with a tray of tea and biscuits. Then, she had whisked the two small boys, Dean and Darren, out from under their parents' feet and taken them to her house for playtime. For many years the boys would go to my parents' house after school until their parents got home from work. Ivy told me that in treating my mother as one of their parents, they were only returning the caring she'd shown them years before.

Gradually, as my mother's health began to change, my trips home became more frequent. She needed more care from social services now that she was housebound. But, within her home she was still up and about, preparing her own meals, reading the daily newspaper and watching the television. We developed a routine of talking on the phone every Sunday morning, and Harry and Ivy let me know if there was a problem. Mother seemed comfortable and content.

One year, as Christmas approached, I called and asked what she would like as a gift.

"I'd like to see you, but I know this is your busy work time. I really don't need anything. Just keep calling me."

On December 17th I flew to London and walked her gift up the path to her. She was delighted and we spent many hours listening to carols, opening the small presents I'd brought her, and retelling stories of

Christmas from my childhood. The time flew. The seven days seemed over before we knew it and there I was, making one last cup of tea for us before I left for the airport. I carried the tray in and set it down near my mother. She lifted her face and looked directly at me.

"Normally, when you go I tell you au revoir. This time, I think I need to tell you adieu."

I stood there silently, looking her in the eyes. I fought to keep back the tears. My mother was brave enough to let me know what she knew. To ensure we left no words unspoken, no regrets.

Slowly, I poured our tea and put her cup next to her bed. Then I walked around and gently swept her into my arms. We hugged long and softly, and she brushed away my tears. She told me to go to the airport, to go back to my home, to my life partner, and that all was well because she knew I was loved. And so I did as I was bid.

WITH THANKS

No collection of family moments is ever complete; there are always additional tales. My hope is that I have given voice to enough spare scenes for the reader to come to know my family.

This collection was made possible by the tireless support of my first writing teachers, Patricia Barry and Dimitri Keriotis; my "Write on Women" writing group: Patricia Harrelson, Shelley Muniz, Cynthia Restivo, Ann St. James, Ellen Stewart, Suzan Still and Christine Taylor; my readers including Carol Biederman; and my editors. Thank you all for your unwavering support.

And for many years of life support, I thank my partner, Rita.

ABOUT THE AUTHOR

Born in Canada, raised in England, Gillian P. Herbert lived in the San Francisco Bay Area for over twenty-five years. For ten years she lived on stunningly beautiful ranch land in the foothills of the Sierras. Now she lives in Portland, Oregon, along with her partner. When not writing, she spends time in her glass studio creating fused glass bowls, platters and restoring stained glass panels.

www.ingramcontent.com/pod-product-compliance
Lightning Source LLC
Chambersburg PA
CBHW021409290426
44108CB00010B/456